THE BIG BOOK OF KUWA

AN EDUCATIONAL COUNTRY TRAVEL PICTURE BOOK FOR KIDS ABOUT HISTORY, DESTINATION PLACES, ANIMALS AND MANY MORE

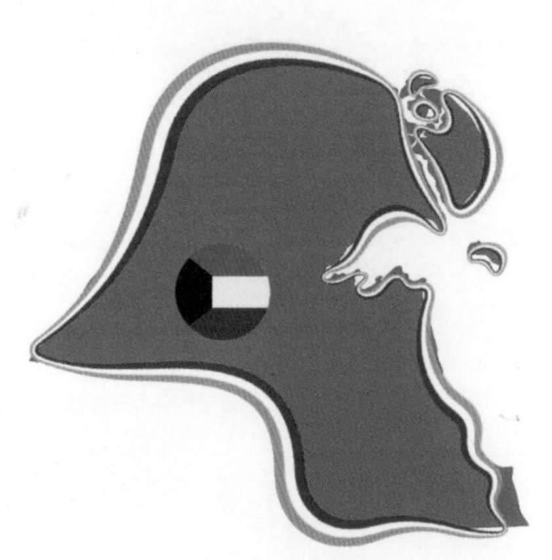

Kuwait is a small country located in the Middle East.

Its capital city is Kuwait City.

What is the national animal of Kuwait?

The national animal of Kuwait is the Arabian camel.

What is the national bird of Kuwait?

The national bird of Kuwait is the Saker falcon.

What is the national sport of Kuwait?

The national sport of Kuwait is football (soccer)

What is the national tree of Kuwait?

The national tree of Kuwait is the Ghaf tree.

What is the official name of Kuwait?

- The official name of Kuwait is the State of Kuwait.

What are the people of Kuwait called?

- The people of Kuwait are called Kuwaitis.

How big is Kuwait?

- Kuwait is 17,820 square kilometers (6,880 square miles) in size.

Which city is the largest in Kuwait?

- The largest city in Kuwait is Kuwait City.

What is the population of Kuwait?

- The population of Kuwait is 4.4 million

Is Kuwait overly populated?

- Yes, Kuwait is considered to be an overpopulated country, with a population density of 248 people per square kilometer (640 people per square mile).

How many governorates does Kuwait have?

- Kuwait has 6 governorates : Al Ahmadi, Al Jahra, Al Farwaniya, Al Kuwait, Hawalli, and Mubarak Al-Kabeer.

What percentage of Kuwait is covered by rainforests?

- Kuwait has 0% rainforest coverage.

What percentage of the world's land does Kuwait occupy?

- Kuwait occupies 0.003% of the world's land.

How many time zones are there in Kuwait?

- Kuwait has 2 time zones: UTC+3 and UTC+4 during summer.

What is Kuwait's nickname?

- Kuwait's nickname is The Pearl of the Gulf.

Who ruled Kuwait first?

- The first ruler of Kuwait was Sabah I bin Jaber

What is the oldest city in Kuwait?

- The oldest city in Kuwait is Kuwait City.

What is the highest temperature ever recorded in Kuwait?

- The highest temperature ever recorded in Kuwait is 54 degrees Celsius (129 degrees Fahrenheit).

What is the lowest temperature ever recorded in Kuwait?

- The lowest temperature ever recorded in Kuwait is -5 degrees Celsius (23 degrees Fahrenheit).

Which months are the coldest in Kuwait?

- The coldest months in Kuwait are December, January, and February.

Which months are the hottest in Kuwait?

- The hottest months in Kuwait are June, July, and August.

What was the old name of Kuwait?

- The old name of Kuwait was Kut, which means "fort" in Arabic and Hindi

Kuwait is known for its vast deserts and beautiful coastline.

The official language of Kuwait is Arabic.

The currency used in Kuwait is the Kuwaiti Dinar (KWD).

Kuwait is one of the richest countries in the world due to its oil reserves.

Oil was discovered in Kuwait in the 1930s, which transformed its economy.

Kuwait has a desert climate, with hot summers and mild winters.

The Kuwait Towers are iconic landmarks in the country and are used for water storage and telecommunications.

The traditional dish of Kuwait is called "Machbous," a rice dish with meat and spices.

Kuwait celebrates its National Day on February 25th.

The Liberation Day in Kuwait is celebrated on February 26th to mark the end of the Gulf War.

Kuwait has a constitutional monarchy with a parliamentary system.

The Emir is the head of state in Kuwait.

The Grand Mosque in Kuwait is one of the largest mosques in the region and can hold thousands of worshipers.

Traditional Kuwaiti clothing includes the "dishdasha" for men and the "abaya" for women.

Pearl diving used to be a major industry in Kuwait before the discovery of oil.

The Kuwaiti flag consists of green, white, red, and black horizontal stripes with a black trapezoid on the hoist side.

The currency of Kuwait, the Kuwaiti Dinar, is one of the highest-valued currencies in the world.

Kuwait is a member of the United Nations and the Arab League.

The Kuwait National Museum showcases the history and culture of the country.

the Kuwaiti coastline extends for about 499 kilometers (310.164 miles).

Kuwait is known for its traditional "souqs" (markets), such as Souq Al-Mubarakiya.

Camels have been historically important animals for transportation and trade in Kuwait's desert.

The Jahra Gate is one of the four remaining historical gates that once guarded the entrances to Kuwait City.

Kuwait has modern infrastructure, including skyscrapers and highways.

Arabic coffee (gahwa) is a popular traditional drink served in Kuwait.

Kuwait has no natural freshwater sources, so desalination plants provide the majority of drinking water.

The Failaka Island in Kuwait was once a trading hub and is now a historical site.

The Al Hamra Tower is the tallest building in Kuwait and one of the tallest sculpted towers in the world.

Traditional Kuwaiti music often features instruments like the oud and tabla.

The date palm tree is significant to Kuwaiti culture, providing shade, food, and materials.

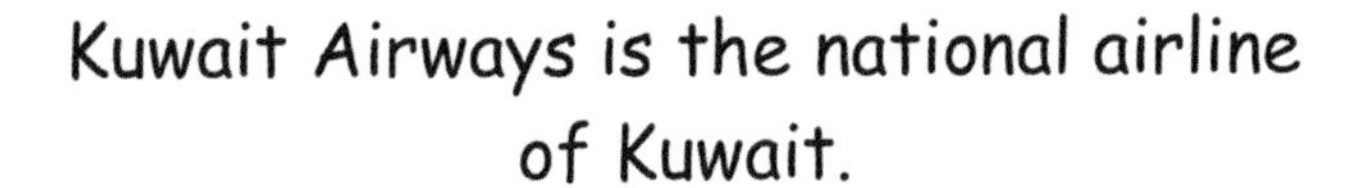

Kuwait has a diverse population with a mix of locals and expatriates from various countries.

Kuwait Airways is the national airline of Kuwait.

The Kuwaiti government offers free education and healthcare to its citizens.

Kuwait has a strong tradition of horse riding and equestrian events.

The country is known for its vibrant traditional dances, like the "Ardha."

The Kuwait Red Crescent Society provides humanitarian aid and relief in times of crisis.

Kuwait hosts various cultural festivals and events throughout the year.

The Liberation Tower is a symbol of Kuwait's liberation from Iraq during the Gulf War.

The Amiri Diwan is the royal palace of the Emir of Kuwait.

Kuwait has a rich tradition of storytelling and folktales.

Kuwait's oil industry was nationalized in the 1970s.

The Al Shaheed Park is a green oasis in Kuwait City with gardens and walking paths.

Kuwaiti women actively participate in the workforce and hold important roles in society.

Kuwaiti architecture often features intricate designs and geometric patterns.

The Arabic language has different dialects spoken across Kuwait.

TOP 15 TRAVEL TIPS FOR VISITING KUWAIT:

- Respect Local Customs: Kuwait is a conservative country with strict Islamic customs. Dress modestly, especially in public areas and religious sites.
- Visa Requirements: Check the visa requirements before traveling to Kuwait. Make sure your passport is valid for at least six months beyond your intended departure date.
- Currency: The official currency is the Kuwaiti Dinar (KWD). Exchange some currency at the airport or local banks upon arrival.
- Language: Arabic is the official language, but English is widely spoken, especially in urban areas and among the expatriate community.
- Local Laws: Familiarize yourself with Kuwait's laws and regulations. Alcohol consumption is illegal, and there are strict penalties for drug offenses.
- Respect for Religion: Kuwait is a Muslim-majority country, so be respectful of Islamic customs. During prayer times, many businesses and restaurants may close briefly.
- Weather: Kuwait has extremely hot summers and mild winters. Plan your visit during the cooler months, between November and April.
- Transportation: Taxis and ride-sharing apps like Uber are common for getting around. Public transportation options are limited, so consider renting a car if needed.
- Safety: Kuwait is generally safe for tourists. However, exercise standard precautions and be aware of your surroundings, especially in crowded areas.
- Health Precautions: Ensure your vaccinations are up-to-date. Tap water is generally safe to drink, but bottled water is widely available.
- Local Cuisine: Don't miss trying traditional Kuwaiti dishes like Machboos (spiced rice with meat) and Gahwa (Arabic coffee). International cuisine is also readily available.
- Shopping: Kuwait offers a variety of shopping experiences, from traditional souqs to modern malls. Bargaining is common in markets.
- Cultural Etiquette: Remove your shoes when entering someone's home and accept offers of food and drink as a sign of hospitality.
- Photography: Always ask for permission before taking photos of people, especially in rural or conservative areas. Avoid taking photos of government or military installations.
- Emergency Numbers: Know the emergency numbers in Kuwait. The general emergency number is 112, and the police emergency number is 112 or 777.